T0152286

GARLIC, MINT, AND SWEET BASIL

Jean-Claude Izzo

GARLIC, MINT, AND SWEET BASIL

Essays on Marseilles, Mediterranean Cuisine, and Noir Fiction

*Translated from the French
by Howard Curtis*

Europa
editions

Europa Editions
214 West 29th Street
New York, N.Y. 10001
www.europaeditions.com
info@europaeditions.com

Copyright © 2013 by Catherine Izzo
First Publication 2013 by Europa Editions
This edition, 2020 by Europa Editions

Translation by Howard Curtis
Translation copyright © 2013 by Europa Editions

Library of Congress Cataloging in Publication Data is available
ISBN 978-1-60945-603-0

Izzo, Jean-Claude
Garlic, Mint, and Sweet Basil

Book design by Emanuele Ragnisco
www.mekkanografici.com

Cover image: Katia Singletary / Alamy Stock Photo

Prepress by Grafica Punto Print – Rome

Printed in the USA

CONTENTS

FABIO MONTALE

GARLIC, MINT, AND SWEET BASIL

INTRODUCTION

MEDITERRANEAN NOIR:
IN PRAISE OF JEAN-CLAUDE IZZO
by Massimo Carlotto

Translated by Michael Reynolds

Recalling the work and the person of Jean-Claude Izzo will forever remain painful for those who knew him. Izzo was first and foremost a good person. It was impossible not to feel warmth for that slight man who always had an attentive, curious look in his eyes and a cigarette in his mouth. I met him in 1995, in Chambéry, during the Festival du Premier Roman. Izzo was there to present *Total Chaos*. I bought the book because its author stirred my interest: he seemed a little detached in many of those cultural gatherings, as if faintly annoyed by them, as he was most certainly annoyed by the quality of food and wine offered by the organizers. I read his book traveling between Chambéry and Turin, where the Salone del Libro was underway. I found it a superb, innovative book, an exemplar in a genre that was finally starting to establish itself here in Italy. I recommended it to my publishers. And not long after, Izzo arrived in Italy. A few sporadic meetings later, I went to Marseilles for a conference. Izzo was not there. He was in hospital. Everyone knew how serious his illness was. Marseilles was rooting for its noirist. Every bookshop in town filled its display windows with Izzo's books. Then, on January 26, Jean-Claude left us. He wasn't even fifty-five.

He left us with many fond memories and several extraordinary novels that convincingly delineated the current now known as "Mediterranean noir".

Autodidact, son of immigrant parents, his father a barman from Naples, his mother a Spanish seamstress. After lengthy battles as a left-wing journalist, having already written for film and television, and author of numerous essays, Izzo decided to take a stab at noir, penning his Marseilles trilogy, *Total Chaos*, *Chourmo*, and *Solea*. The protagonist: Fabio Montale, a cop.

Montale, son of immigrant parents, like Izzo, and child of the inter-ethnic mix that is Marseilles, defiantly stakes out his ground in the city that gave birth to the National Front. In *Solea*, Izzo writes: "It felt good to be in Hassan's bar. There were no barriers of age, sex, color, or class among the regulars there. We were all friends. You could be sure no one who came there for a *pastis* voted for the National Front, or ever had. Not even once, unlike some people I knew. Everyone in this bar knew why they were from Marseilles and not somewhere else, why they lived in Marseilles and not somewhere else. Friendship hung in the air, along with the fumes of anise. We only had to exchange glances to know we were all the children of exiles. There was something reassuring about that. We had nothing to lose, because we'd already lost everything."

Izzo's writing is political, in the tradition of the French neo-polar novels and the writings of Jean-Patrick Manchette. But compared with Manchette, who does not believe in direct political action inasmuch as he believes it is ineffective and doomed to failure, and who limits himself to using noir as an instrument with which to read reality, Izzo goes further. His use of the noir genre is not limited simply to description but penetrates deep into the heart of the incongruities, leaving room for sociological reflection and for a return to his generation's collective memory. Above all, it gives sense to the present day. Via Montale's inner journey, Izzo declares his inexorable faith in the possibility of transformation, both individual and collective. The point that matters most to Izzo, politically speaking, that is, the point that cannot be abandoned, is the existence of a united culture. From the defeats of yesterday come the losers of today. From this perspective, Montale is an extraordinary figure. Child of marginalization, he joins the police so as to avoid the criminal margins. He abandons his group of childhood friends, a group that embodies multiple ethnic differences, but he will never forget his roots. This becomes a source for his feelings of guilt when faced with his role as cop in a society that is becoming increasingly intolerant. Internal gestation and growth obligates him to leave the police force and to become a loner in search of the justice that is not furnished by the courts. What gets him into trouble is the ethic of solidarity and the desire, common to culturally and ethnically mixed milieus, to find a place and a moment in which he can live peacefully.

Izzo considers himself a man of the Mediterranean, with deep roots in the history of this sea he loves to observe from the Sainte Marie lighthouse, but he is above all a Marseillais. He frequently says that Marseilles is his destiny and quotes these lines by Louis Brauquier:

Lost men from other ports,
who carry with you the conscience of the world!

It is not just a question of his passionate love for his city, it is his political conception of belonging to the area of the Mediterranean that leads him to fight against the transformation of Marseilles into a border post between Northern Europe and the countries of the South. The true enemy is the dominant culture of the North, which, starting with the economy, aims to bring about standardization. In his demand for hybridization as the only possible social fabric, Izzo proposes again a Europe born on the shores of the Mediterranean whose only future, to quote Glissant, lies in "Mediterranean Creoleness."

Solea is flamenco music's backbone, but also a piece by Miles Davis. Indeed, music is one of the author's passions. Particularly jazz and the mix of Mediterranean rhythms that characterize contemporary Southern European and North African music. In Izzo's writing, however, music does not simply represent rhythm and a source of nostalgia, but also a key to understanding generational differences. Montano contemplates the merits of rap music. He doesn't like it much, but he reflects: "I was always amazed by the content. How relevant what they said was. How cleverly they used words. What they sang about was the lives of their friends, on the street or in the joint."

With *Solea*, Jean-Claude Izzo gives substance to the political intuition that is the cornerstone of Mediterranean Noir. He understands that the sticking point the movement must face consists in the epochal revolutions that have transformed criminality. Babette Bellini's investigation does not result in the typical affirmation of the Mafia's superiority and organized crime's collusion with higher powers. Izzo defines the outlines of Mediterranean Noir when he introduces into his novel the principal contradiction present in the crime society dyad: "The annual world income of transnational criminal organizations is in the region of a thousand billion dollars, a figure equivalent to the combined gross national product of those countries categorized as low-income." The scale of this mountain of dirty money laundering is at the root of the dizzying increase in the corruption of institutions, of police forces. It is also the catalyst for strategic alliances between entrepreneurs, financial policing bodies, politics, and organized crime. The society in which we live is criminal inasmuch as it produces crime and "anti-crime," resulting in an endless spiral in which legal and illegal economies merge in a single model. Call it, if you will, a socio-economic locomotive, as in the case of northeast Italy.

Mediterranean Noir, in this sense, departs from the existing conception of French Noir, and likewise from the modern police novel. The novel no longer recounts a single "noir" story in a given place at a given moment, but begins with a precise analysis of organized crime.

Another of Izzo's intuitions was his having individuated the Mediterranean as the geographical center of the universal criminal revolution. There is a rich fabric of alliances in this region between new illegal cultures emerging from the east and from Africa. These alliances are influenced by local realities, which they in turn absorb into themselves.

As a result, they possess the means to pursue direct negotiations with established power structures.

This is what Mediterran Noir means: to tell stories with a wide swath; to recount great transformations; to denounce but at the same time to propose the culture of solidarity as an alternative.

THE MEDITERRANEAN
AND ITS NOIR

THE MEDITERRANEAN: POSSIBILITIES FOR HAPPINESS

On his return from Cairo, Flaubert wrote to a friend: "I've come to the conclusion that the things we expect rarely happen." That's the way it often is in the cities of the Mediterranean. You never really find what you came looking for. Maybe because this sea, the ports it gave birth to, the islands cradled by its waters, and the contours of its shores make truth inseparable from happiness. The very intoxication of the light arouses the spirit of contemplation.

I discovered this at home, in Marseilles. Near the Baie des Singes, some distance beyond the little harbor of Les Goudes, at the very eastern end of the city. Hours spent watching the fishing boats returning through the straits of Les Croisettes. It is there, and nowhere else, that they appear to me, and will always appear to me, the most beautiful. I also spent hours watching for that moment, as magical as any, when a cargo ship sails into the light of the sun setting over the sea and disappears for a fraction of a minute. Time enough to believe that anything is possible.

Here, we do not think. Only afterwards. It is afterwards that we dream of all those hours in our lives when we should have learned, and all those when we should have forgotten. Of course, it is unusual for a whole life to go by like this, in contemplation. "The nomad," writes Jean Grenier, "regards the oasis as the Promised Land, and his life is an alternation of grim wandering and bouts of merrymaking. To him, the city is the oasis."

I have travelled like that. From oasis to oasis. From Tangier to Istanbul, from Marseilles to Alexandria, from Naples to Barcelona. And each of these cities, with its narrow, winding streets swarming with people, has offered me its colors, its fruits, its flowers, the gestures of its men and the gaze of its women. Until one day I was able to utter the one essential truth: yes, I love these Mediterranean cities where we feel as if we are carried away.

My Mediterranean is not the one you see on the picture postcards. Happiness is never given, it has to be invented. Not all travelers have the same tastes. Some travel to see, others to enjoy. Still others seek both. But all you need to have done is to have taken, at least once, a bus to a distant oasis, lost in the sands, to know that here, in the Mediterranean, everything will always be given to you, provided you want it, provided you open your eyes and your hands to it.

I arrived in Biskra one evening to find a gentle hot wind, a smell of dust and coffee, the light of a bark fire, the smell of stone and of mutton floating in the air. I made them mine. In this way we lay claim to landscapes.

That is the essential thing when we travel on these shores: to lay claim to what we will never be able to carry away with us, to what exists only in the moment when we look at it and belongs not to our memories but to the joy of living. Small things, like the last quiver of the light before noon. Because, as Leila would say, "life is a fragment of nothing."

I remember one late afternoon in Oran. I had left behind the tumult of the city center to climb the hill of Le Planteur. As far as Santa Cruz. The higher I climbed, the more distant the horizon. The sky opened up. I discovered the city, then the city and the sea, then the city and the sea and the mountain of Tlemcen.

I don't know what I was looking for in Santa Cruz that day. But I liked what I found. Peace. Perhaps because all I had needed to do was close my eyes and the landscape entered into me and became mine, and I realized it would stay inside me wherever I went.

I realized later, in other ports, in other cities of this Mediterranean, that it would always be like this. That what I had discovered was not the pre-packaged Mediterranean sold to us by travel agents and purveyors of easy dreams. That it was just one of the possibilities for happiness that this sea offered. Offered me. Somewhere else, of course, it would have been the same.

And so, over the years, I have created for myself a geography of possibilities for happiness. Byblos is part of this geography. Yazid, a fisherman I met in the little harbor, told me the legend of Adonis. A Phoenician legend. On the first day of spring, Adonis died in the arms of Astarte, at the source of the river that today bears his name. His blood gave birth to the anemones and turned the river rust-red. Astarte's tears rained down on a resurgent nature and brought her lover back to life. A Phoenician temple at the foot of the cave of Afqa pays homage to Astarte.

It was this temple that I had come to see. A temple to love. To fidelity. I was alone. Beirut and its big-city bustle were 25 miles away, and Jounieh, a seaside resort like any other, was just as far. I had barely taken a few steps into the town when, for me, Byblos once again became Gebal, one of the oldest cities in the world.

Yazid did not go with me. That walk to the temple was a solitary one. As were my walks along the Cinque Terre coastline in Liguria, from the Mesco headland to the San Pietro headland. I had let myself be borne along from village to village: Monterosso al Mare, Vernazza, Corniglia, Manarola, Riomaggiore.

Evoking these names was already a joy in itself. You can't get lost in such small villages, and yet that was the true pleasure: to lose yourself in this maze of dark, narrow streets piled one on top of the other, some made entirely of steps.

At a certain point, we know, we will come back to the sea. Inevitably. Each of these villages at the end of five valleys resolutely turns its back on the mountains and faces the Mediterranean. For a long time, it was only possible to reach them by boat. And this memory of the sea is even inscribed on the hulls of the boats, when, upended on the shore to receive a new coat of paint, they reveal shells stuck to their prows.

To get to Manarola, I had taken the Via dell'Amore. The road of love. The only land link between that village and Riomaggiore. A road hollowed out of the rock that falls sheer to the sea, a road that crosses hills covered in vineyards. You feel the desire to caress that nature, even those walls of rock resting in the water.

It was late spring. The hour when the light has not yet grown dense. I was assailed by other images. The Golden Shell of Palermo, where the sun rests all day like a flower in a vase. Djemila, where a heavy, unblemished silence reigns, with that woman running, as in a short story by Camus, toward the starry night that will finally restore her tranquility. Ronda, the Andalucian mountain city hanging in the sky, which even cured Rainer Maria Rilke's depression. The blue bay of Salamis, when you discover it from the Philopappos Monument, between bare hills and the stony plain.

I searched with my eyes for the island of Elba, and other islands emerged. The volcano of Santorini, which rises from the sea with the transparency of glass. Cape Sounion, and the tiny Psara, swept by the dust and the winds, Symi, the island of sponges, clinging to Mount Siglos.

This Italian land suddenly spoke to me in Greek. Doubtless because in Greece, as Jean Grenier has written, there is a "friendship between minerals and man." And the Mediterranean is nothing other than an appeal to their reconciliation.

There, gazing lovingly around, I remember telling myself that there is nothing more beautiful, more significant, for anyone who loves Africa and the Mediterranean with the same love, than contemplating their union in this sea. When, that evening, I got back to Vernazza, the village flag, with its Arab crescent moon, merely confirmed it. At that point, the only thing remaining was to go to the

Princes' Islands, a stone's throw from Istanbul. Kizil Adalar—"the Red Islands" in Turkish. There, I discovered the limpid waters of the creek of Kalpazankaya. But I didn't travel there only to bathe in the sea, or even to eat the most delicious tandoor kebab—mutton roasted in a clay oven. I went there for the sheer pleasure of knowing that I was between two waters, between two worlds. Between East and West.

LISTENING TO THE SEA

From Marseilles, I look at the world. It is from here—at the top of the steps that lead up to the Sainte-Marie lighthouse, at the eastern end of the sea wall—that I think of the world. Of the distant world, of the world nearby. That I think of myself too. Mediterranean. A Mediterranean man.

Marseilles is 2,600 years old. I belong to that history. I am in that history. I am in this minor century and sea, as the Neapolitan writer Erri de Luca so rightly calls it. Marseilles is my destiny, like the Mediterranean. Yes, that is what I declare as I gaze out at the open sea, my back up against the hot stone of the Sainte-Marie lighthouse, my head full, as always, of the poetry of Louis Brauquier:

> *Lost men from other ports,*
> *who carry with you the conscience of the world!*

Marseilles exists only in these words. All the rest is just hot air. Political, or economic. Cultural too, sometimes. If we forget that, we die.

Wherever I go these days, the word on everyone's lips is

Europe. That's why I come to the Saint-Marie lighthouse. It's enough to make you despair. Because I don't see any European future for Marseilles. In spite of what they say. Marseilles is a Mediterranean city. And the Mediterranean has two shores. Not just ours. Today, Europe only talks of one, and France is all too ready to fall in line. Making this sea, for the first time, a border between East and West, North and South. Separating us from Africa and Asia Minor.

On behalf of the lost Andalucias, the silent Alexandria, the divided Tangier, the massacred Beirut, we ought to remember that European culture was born on the shores of the Mediterranean, in the Middle East. Europa, lest we forget, was a Phoenician goddess abducted by Zeus!

Forgive me, but I can't rid myself, when I talk about Marseilles, of this fear of being marginalized. Just as the cultures of central Europe are already marginalized. The philosopher Predrag Matvejevi writes: "Our century is coming to an end marked by 'ex-worlds': ex-communist, ex-Soviet, ex-Yugoslav." Tomorrow, the Mediterranean may well be one of these "ex"es. And Marseilles with it.

From the Sainte-Marie lighthouse, I do not turn my back on the city, no, on the contrary, I lean over her. And I look at the sea. The open sea.

That horizon from which one day the boat of a Phocaean named Protis emerged.

Protis is our Ulysses, the Ulysses of Marseilles. I assume that before dropping anchor here he had travelled for many years, known many countries and met many Calypsos. The legend does not say whether there was a

Penelope waiting for him in his country. It simply recalls that a young girl from this region, Gyptis, handed him a glass of cold water and chose him as her husband.

The myth has no meaning unless we read it for what it is. And unless it becomes a project. Marseilles proudly proclaims its experience of the world. We might add: its Mediterranean experience. Because we have no other. But could we ever have any other? That is the question I ask, as a bastard from Marseilles, a half-breed product of Italian, Spanish and Arab cultures. And although I may be a French citizen today, the sea—this Mediterranean of ours, on which my eyes, my heart and my thoughts are focused—remains the only place where I feel that I exist. Where I can envisage a future for myself. In spite of everything. That is how much trust I have in Marseilles. Marseilles. The one true survivor of the worlds of the Mediterranean will, I hope, be able to avoid becoming the border post—a modern version of the Roman Empire's *limes*—between the civilized world and the barbarian world, between Northern Europe and the countries of the South, as advocated in a World Bank report to the European elites.

Yes, I believe, as I look at the sea, that there is a future for Europe, and beauty in that future. It lies in what Edouard Glissant calls "Mediterranean Creoleness."

Those are the stakes. The choice between the old economic, separatist, segregationist way of thinking (of the World Bank and international private capital) and a new culture, diverse, mixed, where man remains master both of his time and of his geographical and social space.

This I demand. All this. Out of loyalty to the first two lovers of Marseilles, Gyptis and Proteus. In other words, out of love.

I Am at Home Everywhere

You may be surprised to hear this, but I am not a traveler. I am a child of migration. My father, having met a beautiful woman from Seville, halted on his road of exile. In Marseilles. I could have been born somewhere else, like my cousins. In Buenos Aires, or New York. Or else in Canada, where my parents dreamed of going to live soon after the war. It wouldn't have made any difference. Here or elsewhere, I would have been the son of an exile. That is my only baggage. My only inheritance. My memory. And therefore my story. That means that the blood that courses through my veins does not belong to one race, one country, one land. Or even one nation. One day I will have to explain all this, better maybe than I have done in my novels. Telling the itineraries of my old friends, Armenians and Greeks, Spaniards and Gypsies, also children of migration. To be "from somewhere else" changes everything. You look at the world in a different way. I mean that wherever I am, I am at home. Even in those countries whose language I do not know. I just have to read a travel story or a novel by a writer to make his territory, his memories, my own. And become his twin. I had this sensation for the first time when I read *Wedding in Tipasa* by Camus. I felt as if I was an Algerian. I felt a passionate need for Algeria. Not long after that, I found myself in Ethiopia. In Hara, to be exact. In the footsteps of Rimbaud. There, I learned the freedom of wandering, of moving from place to place not to discover, to meet, to learn, but to merge into the Other, and see through his eyes "the other world," the one from which you come. And so I became an Ethiopian. I was an Egyptian one night in Cairo. I've been a Turk sometimes. But also Irish, and Argentinian out of love. Often I am still Italian or Spanish. And if it's true that I have been so many other nationalities, today I dream of being Laotian, and sometimes also Japanese, thanks to a writer named Haruki Murakami. There are times, I must say, when I no longer know if I have lived in Havana, in Bali, in Missoula or in Shanghai, or if I've simply read too much Cendrars, Hemingway, Luis Sepúlveda, Jim Harrison and James Crumley, Vicki Baum, Stevenson, Melville, Conrad, and Pierre MacOrlan, whom nobody reads these days. None of this really matters, when you come down to it. Truth and falsehood. Imagination is a reality, sometimes more real than reality itself. Conrad could explain that better than I can. The importance of allowing reality to find its own logic.

All too often we do not dare go deep enough into ourselves. We meet the gaze of the Other as an invitation. But we remain on the dock. Because the dock is the safest thing that exists, isn't it? Terra firma. The earth, reminding us that we are from here, from one country, one race, one nation. We are partial to docks when we have a set reason to be there. A journey. A vacation. For a specific time. With a guidebook in our hands and a return ticket in our pockets. We know that we are leaving and that we will come back, of course, to the same dock. It is often at that moment that we look away from the Other. And that he becomes a stranger to us. Hostile. A stranger is necessarily hostile to the country, the race, the nation to which we claim out loud to belong. I don't know if you've followed me so far. I like to think you have. I also like to think that there is no point going anywhere else if we do not recognize ourselves in the eyes of the Other. That, I think, is why most tourist resorts resemble fortified camps. We don't try to meet the Other. We only want what belongs to him. His sea, his beaches, his palm trees. All these things I learned from my father.

And Marseilles completed my education. Beyond the horizon, toward which I looked from the end of the sea wall, down in the harbor, I knew that I had cousins, with their many children. They are still out there somewhere, but I no longer know where. On which side of the barbed wire that divides Cyprus between Greeks and Turks? On which hypothetical border in Rwanda? In which nation of the former Yugoslavia? Or in which unsanitary gypsy camp at the gates of the city? It's when I think about them that my feet start to itch, and I take out my cardboard suitcase and dream of setting off. To go and meet them, and share what we have in common, the pleasure of the universe. The pleasure I taste when, at home, in the still air of summer and noon, I read Louis Owens and put myself in the shoes of an Indian.

I dream of wide open spaces. I reinvent the meaning of the earth. And then I remember a civilized people once saying that the only good Indian is a dead Indian, and realize that I'm shivering, because on the road of exile the weather is cold.

THE BLUE AND THE BLACK

In the beginning is the Book. And that moment in which Cain kills his brother Abel. In the blood of this fratricide, the Mediterranean gives us the first noir novel.

There may well have been other murders before this, but this one is written down, and establishes forever the singular problem of mankind: that crime is the driving force that, over the centuries, will govern relationships between people. Whoever they are. Masters or servants. Princes or emperors. Free men or slaves. In the beginning, indeed, all the motives for murder already existed. Envy, jealousy. Desire, fear. Money. Power. Hatred. Hatred of others. Hatred of the world.

That is the basis of all the Greek tragedies. In case we had forgotten, the chutzpah of Patrick Raynal, editor of Gallimard's *Série noire*, was there to remind us. When he published Sophocles's *Oedipus Rex* in his famous series, some in the narrow circles of the publishing world thought he was joking. But he wasn't. Far from it.

It was an academic, Didier Malmaison, who adapted the Greek text into a *Série noire* novel. This magnificent book, which opens with a classic noir scene—a stranger arrives in town, everyone watches him, closing their doors and windows as he passes, he crosses the street—can be read in one sitting. Like a real crime novel. "Well, if you look at it that way . . . " many teachers were forced to admit. Indeed, if you look at it that way, the line of descent from Greek tragedy to the noir novel becomes obvious. In Oedipus we witness a search for the truth of a man's life. In the noir novel, beginning with the Americans, the same process is developed, in parallel with an investigation into the social conditions of contemporary man, the modern form of fate. This is very clear in the works of David Goodis and Jim Thompson, who both deal with the tragedy of modern societies.

In a 1995 interview appearing in the review *Les Temps Modernes*, Patrick Raynal explained this lineage: "If we can broadly define noir writing, noir inspiration, as a way of looking at the world, at the dark opaque criminal side of the world, shot through with the intense feeling of fatality we carry within us due to the fact that the only thing we know for certain is that we are going to die, then *Oedipus* can indeed be said to be the first noir novel."

James M. Cain, in *The Postman Always Rings Twice*, is another exponent of modern tragedy. I have not plucked Cain's name from the air. We now know that his work was a major influence on Albert Camus's *The Outsider*. The similarities are striking. A man, in no way predisposed to become a criminal, kills another man and finds himself in prison. Beneath "the stars in the night sky," he discovers the "benign indifference of the world," and his last wish, in order for the drama to be fully consummated, is "that there should be a crowd of spectators at [his] execution and that they should greet [him] with cries of hatred."

For me, *The Outsider* is the beginning of the modern Mediterranean crime novel. More so, in my opinion, than the novels of Manuel Vázquez Montalbán, who owes more, in both form and content, to Chandler and Hammett than to Cain. Today, there are many authors continuing this line of descent from Greek tragedy. The Spaniards Andreu Martín and Francisco Gonzales Ledesma, the Italians Peppe Ferrandino, Nino Filasto, Santo Piazzese, Nicoletta Vallorani and Carlo Lucarelli, the Algerians Yasmina Khadra and Abdelkader Djemaï, and the Frenchmen René Frégni, Pascal Dessaint and Marcus Malte. All of them combine the viewpoint of Camus with that of Montalbán. The inspiration comes from this observation by Camus, in *Helen's Exile* (1948): "Such moments make one realize that if the Greeks knew despair, they experienced it always through beauty and its oppressive quality. In this golden sadness, tragedy reaches its highest point. The despair of our world, on the other hand, has fed on ugliness and crisis. For which reason, Europe would be ignoble, if ever suffering could be." The Mediterranean crime novel is the fatalistic acceptance of this drama that has hung over us ever since man killed his brother on one of the shores of this sea.

Individual tragedy is echoed in the collective tragedy of the Balkans and Algeria, where the same dark blood flows. Faced with these conflicts which have punctuated the history of the Mediterranean, artists have tirelessly responded with their passion for the unifying sea. Paraphrasing

Camus, I would call it a recognition of our ignorance, a rejection of fanaticism and of the limits of the world and of man, the beloved face, and finally beauty: that is the theatre in which we play out the same drama as the Greeks. And along with the other authors of these two shores, I affirm here, in the Mediterranean, in the name of a blue Mediterranean against a black Mediterranean, that the meaning of the history of tomorrow is not what we think. Far from it.

MARSEILLES

MARSEILLES IS IN MY HEART

I was born in Marseilles. Of an Italian father and a Spanish mother. One of those crossbreeds to whom this city holds the secret. Nobody is ever born in Marseilles by chance. Marseilles is, and has always been, the port of exiles, of Mediterranean exiles, of exiles from our former colonial routes. Here, whoever disembarks in the port is inevitably at home. Wherever you are from, you feel at home in Marseilles. You see familiar faces on the streets, you smell familiar smells. Marseilles is familiar. From the moment you first look at her.

That is why I love this city, my city. She is beautiful because of that familiarity, which is like bread to be shared by all. She is beautiful only because of her humanity. The rest is just chauvinism. There are plenty of beautiful cities with beautiful monuments in Europe. The world is full of beautiful harbors, beautiful bays, magnificent ports. I am not a chauvinist. I am Marseillais. That means I am from here, passionately so, and from everywhere else at the same time. Marseilles is my world culture. My initial world education.

It is through those ancient navigation routes toward the

East, Africa, then toward the Americas, those routes that are real to some of us, and merely dreamed about by most people, that Marseilles lives, wherever we go. Paris is an attraction. Marseilles is a passport. When I am far from her, which I often am, I think of Marseilles, without homesickness. But with the same emotion we feel for a beloved woman whom we have left behind to go traveling, and whom we desire more intensely to see again as the days pass.

I think about that, about all the things I have learned on the streets of Marseilles, all the things that stick to my skin: hospitality, tolerance, respect for others. Uncompromising friendship and that essential quality of love: loyalty. And, paraphrasing my friend from L'Estaque, the film director Robert Guédiguian, I will say: Marseilles is my identity, my culture and my morality. And, whether I am here or elsewhere, when I speak the language of my home, I reinvent the language that Gyptis, the Ligurian Celt, and Protis, the Phocaean from Asia Minor, invented during their night of love, 2,600 years ago. A language in which every letter of the alphabet has to be profoundly human. I say there is no risk in speaking that language. Only happiness.

I like to think—given that I grew up here—that Marseilles, my city, is not a goal in itself but only a door open to the world, and to other people. A door that must remain open forever.

I Like to Feel Marseilles
Pulsating Beneath my Tongue

Marseilles is not Provençal, and never has been.

In most restaurants, we eat simple, inexpensive, unpretentious dishes, not according to a tradition, but out of a fierce loyalty to our origins.

As many people have said: there is no innovation in the cuisine of Marseilles, no fusion, just self-perpetuation. Eating takes us back to our countries. To sit down to a meal, whether at home or in a restaurant, with our families or with our friends, is to recover our memories.

So I won't talk about Provençal cuisine.

That means finally sweeping away all the equivocal remarks made about Marseilles and its cuisine. A city where, supposedly, people eat, if not badly, at least never very well. And where, it is often said, there is a desperate lack of imagination. I even read one day that we should invent a bouillabaisse tagine! Why not, if there are people who like that kind of thing? But it makes me smile, because if such a thing doesn't already exist, it must be because it has no reason to exist. Let me make myself clear: I belong to this city and, to be honest, I often get more pleasure eating a slice of pizza from Roger and Nanette's, looking out to sea with my backside on a rock, than having to face the boredom of sole Napoleon in olive *jus* at a padded restaurant crowded with those who dream of a different city. A homogeneous city, devoid of passion and of course without exuberance. A civilized Provençal city, I suppose. Where garlic would be carefully rationed, even banned from noontime meals—those famous business lunches where people peck at their food rather than eat it. When I eat, I like to feel Marseilles pulsating beneath my tongue. Wild and common, the way sea bass can be, or white bream, or mullet grilled with fennel and lightly sprinkled with olive oil, the kind you find Chez Paul or at L'Oursin. In other words, the restaurants where I like hanging out are rarely mentioned in guidebooks and never win awards. Who cares? The people you might come across in certain places are not necessarily those I want to rub shoulders with. Such people aren't too crazy about aïoli, bouillabaisse or anchovy purée. They don't know anything about the pleasure of fried chickpea cakes. They've never tasted snails in spicy sauce, or sea urchins, or lambs' feet and tripe, or cod in a tomato and red wine sauce, or eggplant ratatouille or fresh bean stew, and they don't know the joy of feasting on slightly warm vegetable soup with basil and garlic in the shade of a pine. I haven't plucked these dishes out of thin air. The cuisine of Marseilles has always rested on the art of using fish and vegetables disdained by the local ship-owning upper classes, who were kept supplied with refined produce like game and poultry, lamb, truffles, cheese, and fruit by the farms of the Aix region. That was how bouillabaisse was born: out of the ugly looking, inedible, unsellable scorpion fish. There are many other examples. A poor man's cuisine, yes, but one whose genius still delights us, even if these days people argue over the thousand and one ways to prepare bouillabaisse. In order not to upset anyone, I'll only say that it's best to prepare it yourself. But it's the same with all Marseilles recipes, and more broadly with the dishes of the Mediterranean: couscous, tagine, paella, or a simple pasta in sauce with meatballs and slices of veal. And through them we discover all the conviviality of the South, where eating is a celebration. When I find myself in a restaurant, that's what I look for above all: a family atmosphere. It's true that the daily dishes may not be on a par with those at Chez Étienne, in the Panier. But that's a bit like life itself. You take what the day serves up. You know that one day something miraculous is going to come your way. It couldn't be otherwise. And when it does you will be struck dumb by ravioli in olive purée, calamari in parsley, or even just a little fried fish. Nothing more. That's how I like Marseilles.

GARLIC

The first girl I ever kissed smelled of garlic. It was in a hut in Les Goudes, at that hour on a summer's day when adults take an afternoon nap. I learned, that year I turned fifteen, to love garlic. Its smell in the mouth. Its taste on the tongue. And the intoxication of kisses, of pleasure. Then came the joys of bread simply rubbed in garlic and the spicy bodies of women. Since then, in my kitchen, garlic has reigned supreme. In spite of its bad reputation. Because garlic, as you must have realized by now, is part of our hunger for life. It is garlic alone that opens the doors to all flavors. It knows how to welcome them. That's what cooking and eating is: a welcome. Lovers, friends, children, grandchildren. All of us, without exception, around the table, peeling white or red beans, cutting eggplant and zucchini and green and red and yellow peppers, gutting fish, washing octopus and squid and cuttlefish, cutting up rabbit, marinating red meat . . . Sea bream in fennel, aïoli, ratatouille, bouillabaisse, vegetable soup, paella, braised artichoke in white wine broth, cod in tomato and red wine sauce . . . These dishes are born out of friendship, out of the pleasure of being together, unrestrained words and laughter. And the house is filled with a strong odor. A bold, wild odor. Because it's obvious that cooking with garlic is a culinary outrage, an insult to good taste. It is in these gestures around garlic that worlds divide. More seriously than you might imagine. Nothing, in fact, goes better with garlic than wine, preferably red wine. Bandol in particular, from the wonderful Mourvèdre grape. Generous, elegant, powerful, rich, aromatic wines. With each mouthful, the garlic and wine together push the outrage to its limits, until the palate can't take it anymore. Like the intoxication of a first kiss. That's why I say, in opposition to all the bloodsucking vampires who steal our energy, empty our brains, and dry our hearts: Eat garlic and drink wine. That's life. Because, to paraphrase the writer Jim Harrison, it's hard to get by in this life without garlic and wine.

MINT

We love mint for its smell. It's the most popular. Ask us to name a plant that smells good and it is mint, and only mint, that comes to mind. Its scent, it must be admitted, though slightly peppery, does not go to our heads, does not intoxicate. What moves us is its grace. And we simply have to drop a few leaves into a teapot to be transported to the Palace of Scheherazade.

That is how mint works. Like a love potion. I will even say that it opens the gates to that Orient of the imagination where, as Baudelaire sang, all is luxury, calm, and voluptuousness.

Perhaps that is why mint is used so little in Western cooking, even in the South. Because of the fear of traveling, which takes us far from Penelope more than it returns us to her. But, you will say, we drink mint. Don't make me laugh. The thing we add to water when we're on vacation, to color it green, has long forgotten its origins! Teenagers may still believe that if we drink a lot of it we'll become amorous, but in fact it has no effect on human beings. Besides, I have never yet known a man or a woman who, having drunk mint in water all summer, has ever cried out, "Get up and come with me: we will renounce our royal power and travel the vast world, thinking of nothing but love . . . "

If I may be allowed a piece of advice, spread mint about you. Corsican mint to decorate your garden paths with its tiny mauve flowers. Orange mint with leaves veined in red. Pennyroyal mint, whose small pink flowers grow between the flagstones. Banana mint with its pale green leaves dotted with cream and white. Last but not least, green mint in pots on your windowsills. Breathe in those peppery smells. Then you will discover that there are always 1001 nights to your dreams. And you will cherish mint as the most beautiful of lovers.

I grew up with the smell of basil. Like all children of the South. Whenever my mother came back from the market, she always brought two or three pots of it with her, which she placed on the windowsill in the kitchen. That was the place for basil. In the shade of the shutters, left half open as soon as spring arrived. I learned later that its smell frightened away insects. Later still, I learned many other things. For example, that until the Revolution basil was a royal plant. It could only be gathered with a gold billhook, and only by a person of high rank. But I don't suppose the plebs waited for Year One of the Republic to sprinkle it on their food! Good taste and good smells are acquired instinctively and, once you have sniffed basil, it's something you can't do without. That's how it is for me. Whenever I can't smell it in my house, I miss it. With the arrival of the first tomato, I need it. A few drops of olive oil on nice red *pomodori*, two or three leaves of basil sprinkled over it, a hunk of leftover bread rubbed in garlic, and your taste buds go dancing! I don't know any simpler happiness. The first one offered by basil. The others will tempt you. Such as, once the meal is over, simply closing the shutters on the afternoon heat. Remembering the pot of basil on the windowsill of your room. In the scented shade of the room, life becomes simpler. Like the pleasure of loving. Have no fear: an excess of basil, like an excess of love, will not damage the heart.

HERE, MY DARLING, TASTE THIS

Wherever I go, in any city in the world, the first thing I do is go to the market. To feel the city. I was brought up that way, with that tradition of going to the market. Every day. Marseilles had as many markets as it had neighborhoods and squares. We used to live near one of the most popular streets in the city. The market on Rue-Longue-des-Capucines was not a Provençal market, it was a Mediterranean market. Where the humblest cucumber already savored the joy of being prepared in an Eastern way or a Latin way. Fruit and vegetables, but also herbs and spices. The variety of colors rivaled the multiplicity of smells. Mingling with the cries and the laughter. Words exchanged amid the noise and bustle: "Fire! Fire! My watermelon's on fire!" Spoken in that drawling accent that takes time to say things. "Here, my darling, taste this!"

That was where I discovered the wonders of the world, and there were a lot more than seven. Like olives. There wasn't just one or two, black or green, but whole stalls of olives, from different places, prepared and seasoned for all the palate's revolutions. "Taste this, son, just take it . . . " The intoxication of living was invented here.

And is constantly invented in markets. That's what I tell myself whenever I while away my time like this, even when I am far from home. In another port. Another city. A village. There is a feeling of community that is born as soon as you stroll around a market. Like a common appetite for living. The eyes say it. The smiles, too. Dinner time will be soon. The magic hour for cooking fresh food. According to mood. And our desires. For the family, and for others, this cuisine is one of conviviality. Of togetherness. *Antipasti* with tagine, eggplant with couscous, spaghetti *vongole* with stuffed vine leaves, bouillabaisse with meze. I remember that I always tried to imagine what my mother was making us to eat from the vegetables she had chosen. White beans, red beans, green beans meant vegetable soup. Carrots, cauliflower, and green beans meant aïoli. Purple artichokes meant *barigoule*. Tomatoes and zucchini and eggplant meant *petit-farcis*. Of course, there was always a mystery about certain vegetables that could be used in several dishes. Leeks, broad beans, broccoli, peas, fennel, tomatoes . . . As I grew up, I learned, for example, that each of the varieties of tomato had its use: for salads, for coulis, or for *farcis*. "Here, taste this," my mother would say, coming back from the market. She would hold up one of the tomatoes, cut in two, with a trickle of olive oil on it. I loved pendelotte tomatoes. They reminded me of Italy, where we went on vacation. But what was true for the tomato was also true for any other young vegetable. That was something I discovered later. Along with the pleasure of wines. And the pleasure of olive oil. This is where you find the basis of taste. In these ordinary markets which are the soul of a city. Where the influences of the South inspire recipes, while escaping those who would like to set them in stone. The years have passed. I still go to markets. And always, like Prévert, I want to make an inventory of them. Beginning with those intoxications of the senses: basil, savory, dill, tarragon, parsley, marjoram, mint, rosemary, sage, thyme, aniseed. Their smell makes your mouth water. Cooking is something we dream, first of all. Before we do it. It invites us. As Manuel Vázquez Montalbán has taught us: we can cook to perpetuate, but also to seduce. It is afterwards, when we are at the table, indulging in the intoxication of all these tastes of sun-ripened produce, that a multitude of tiny details comes back to our eyes and ears: the noise of a fountain in a little square, the smell of warmed tiles, the shady silence of an alleyway . . . The sweetness of living? The sensuality would be more accurate. I am always taken by surprise in a market—how can we not be filled with wonder at a tiny stall of zucchini flowers? Then I reason with myself. The only thing that matters is the essential, not the superfluous. And the only thing that exists here is the pleasure of the day. Tomorrow belongs to tomorrow and is quite another story. That is the happiness of the Mediterranean, a way of giving meaning to each day, day after day. Shopping in a market is nothing but the reinvention of the art of living simply and together.

M<small>ARSEILLES</small>: A M<small>USICAL</small> T<small>RADING</small> P<small>OST</small>

One day when I was a little boy, I was on my way to see my cousins in the Panier when music filled the steps of the Montée des Accoules. A song in Spanish. A tango. I discovered later that it was *Garufa* by Edmundo Rivero. But the name of the singer didn't matter. What struck me was that when I turned right onto Rue du Refuge, I heard the unforgettable voice of Reinette l'Oranaise, and at the end of the street a man leaning out of a window was humming *Maruzzella, Marruzella*. Renato Carosone. My father used to listen to him at home. He bought every new 45 rpm as if it was the latest news from his family in Naples. On Rue des Pistoles, where my grandmother lived, both sides of the street were the kingdom of flamenco, mostly Arab-Andalucian. Subsequently, I found a similar atmosphere on the streets of Barcelona, near the Plaza Real. Then in Genoa. And also in Algiers. It was there that I first heard *Bambino* in Arabic. By Lili Boniche. The shores of the Mediterranean were joining together. They still do. Even today, when the Catalan Lluis Llach "hands over" to the Moroccan Amina Alaoui and the Greek Nena Venetsanou in *Un pont de mar blava*. I like to believe that it will always be this way. On both shores of the Mediterranean. That our shores will still join together. And that they will remain without borders, as Louis Brauquier wrote in the *Cahiers du Sud*.

I haven't plucked the name of that famous review, born in Marseilles, out of the air, nor that of Brauquier, one of this city's finest poets.

Today, Marseilles has a curious tendency to close her doors and windows. Refusing to sing about herself on her hybrid shores. Thinking that certain kinds of music have too much flavor, too much smell, even, like our markets. Asserting that what comes from elsewhere has no reason to be here, and that there is no other shore to the Mediterranean but our own. Latin, obviously. Harping on about our roots in the land, in the hills of Provence, where you can't see the sea, where you don't even dream of the sea. And which echo, when Sunday comes, to the fifes and drums so beloved of Frédéric Mistral.[1]

And at the same time, we are expected to take sides: either Vincent Scotto or Khaled.[2] But what nobody can deny, unless they are of bad faith, is that Marseilles is not one, but multiple. It is multicultural, multiracial, and, of course, multi-musical. The people of Marseilles sing in several languages, just as we think and dream in several languages. And love too.

[1] Frédéric Mistral, 1830–1914: writer and poet, winner of the Nobel Prize in 1904. Widely considered the most revered and acclaimed writer in Occitan literature.
[2] Vincent Scotto, 1874 (Marseilles)—1952 (Paris): French composer. Khaled, b. 1960 (Oran, Algeria) is a raï singer-songwriter.

Marseilles the capital, where Verdi is as popular as Bob Marley. That, I think, is what makes groups like IAM or Massilia Sound System so intelligent: the fact they have understood that. Both come from this music of our childhood, and both have inherited these songs, these different kinds of music that their fathers hummed and that lingered on the streets of Marseilles.

It should be clear by now that, for me, the groups, the kinds of music, the albums that are born in this city—rap, raï, ragga, but also Brazilian music, flamenco jazz, accordion tunes—are to music what the *Cahiers du Sud* was to literature. These different kinds of music help us to hear ourselves. Each group—those that grew in the neighborhoods of the city, those that come here to play—is also a wager. Not only cultural. A wager for humanity. And therefore for the future. A wager similar to that of the *Cahiers du Sud*, when it defied Vichy and Nazi censorship and published—in Algeria, lest we forget—*Exile* by St. John Perse.

There, just a few miles from Marseilles, writers are banned by the city's libraries. There, too, one night's boat ride from Marseilles, musicians are killed on the street. While the shores of the Mediterranean sing and dance in Marseilles, and their languages mingle, and their roots with them, political and religious fundamentalism shakes its death rattle.

In Marseilles, of course, we carry on regardless. We know perfectly well that it is our sea that unites us. And that our South, to quote Brauquier again, is "an attempt to point the way toward those vague regions where man situates his paradise."

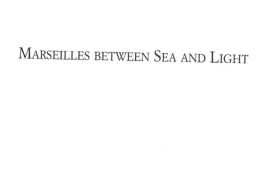

Marseilles between Sea and Light

It was September, but it could have been July. Marseilles's glorious summer was not yet over. In the noisy streets, as exuberant as those of all southern cities, the fierce August forest fires in Septème-les-Vallons, Le Rove, and Allauch, and everyone's unspoken fear of seeing the flames engulf the city, had been forgotten. That evening, Olympique Marseilles was playing Bordeaux. In Bordeaux. From eight in the evening, the neighborhood bars would be filled with supporters. People here like to go to bars to watch soccer matches. One or two TV sets, depending on the bar. Some men even bring their wives and kids. A slice of pizza, a beer, and ninety minutes spent hoping for your club's victory. Each bar is like a microcosm of the stadium and, apart from Paris-Saint-Germain, if you come from somewhere else or are simply passing through the city you can demonstrate your support for the opposing team. Within limits, of course. We have our honor, all the same!

For the moment, in the Vieux Port, on the terrace of the Samaritaine, we drink in for as long as possible, in the same carefree manner as always, that superb autumn light pouring down from the sky after five in the afternoon. You can't understand anything about this city if you are indifferent to her light. It is tangible, even when the heat is at its most intense. When it forces you to lower your eyes. Marseilles is a city of light. And of wind, that famous mistral that rushes in from the top of her alleyways and sweeps everything down to the sea. As far as the open sea off the Frioul Islands, Pomègues, and Ratonneaux. Even past Planier, the now extinguished lighthouse that has become a diving school, which used to indicate to all the sailors in the world that Marseilles was within reach, and that her women, whether or not they were whores, would make them forget their passion for distant seas and islands. Marseilles, to tell the truth, can only be loved like that, arriving by sea. Early in the morning. At the hour when the sun, rising behind the massif of Marseilleveyre, embraces her hills and turns her old stones pink. Then you see Marseilles just as Protis the Phocean discovered her. And who cares if this is an exaggeration? Marseilles always exaggerates. That is her essence. And basically nothing has changed since that day. You just have to arrive by ferry from Corsica to relive that story. Or, even more simply, to come back from a night's fishing off l'Estaque. When the harbor opens its arms to you, then and only then you discover the eternal meaning of this city: Hospitality. Marseilles gives herself without resistance to those who know how to take her and love her. Marseilles is a myth. That is the only thing there is to see. To embrace. The rest can be as futile or vain as anywhere else. We might even say that the city is just like those fake blondes you meet on her streets. They display only what they are not. Second Empire vanities like the colonial wealth of the Palais du Pharo, with its magnificent view of the bay and the city, and the Palais Longchamp, which towers over her but whose avenue, leading to the sea, loses itself in a maze of alleyways forgotten by everyone. The futility of the renovation and restoration of the neighborhood of the Grands Carmes and the old neighborhood of the Panier, where the new Italian-style ocher façades try to make everyone forget the ancient roots of the city, which are Greek, and therefore tragic, drowned now beneath tons of concrete to create shopping malls and parking garages, obliterating all maritime, Oriental and adventurous daydreams. Charles de Gaulle against Pytheas: Pytheas who revolutionized geography by discovering the route to the poles and disproving Strabo. That may well be why the Garden of the Vestiges, behind the Bourse shopping mall, a stone's throw from the Vieux Port, is the saddest place in Marseilles. It is here, faced with a few heaped-up stones, fragments of Greek or Roman fortifications, that the memory of the city is lost. Beauty has been exiled. The Greeks, from whom the Marseillais claim inspiration, took up arms for beauty. The beauty of Helen. And so, in our frustration, we take the ferry. The *Marius*, in tribute to Pagnol and Raimu. Making another attempt to understand this city, by linking the Quai de la Marine to the Quai de Rive Nueve. Atypical is not the word for Marseilles. Unconventional is more accurate. Like the Saint-Charles station. With its monumental staircases turned toward the city and its magnificent facade looking toward the harbor, the sea, the East. The journey is a brief one. From the Place de la Mairie to the Place aux Huiles. There, on the quayside, stands the statue of Vincent Scotto, who sang of the working class of Marseilles and made it sing. We can make the journey again. In the other direction. It is as we go from one dock to the other, our eyes turned now toward the open sea, now toward the Canebière, that this city reveals herself. That we understand, finally, that we have to let ourselves be carried away by her, by her streets and hills, all of them so built-up that we forget that Marseilles is made up of hills descending toward the sea. Could anyone coming to Marseilles, and going up Rue de la République with its Haussmann-style buildings—it stretches from the Vieux-Port to the commercial port of La Joliette—ever imagine that this street was bored through a hill by Napoleon III's town planners? The hill of the Carmes. No, of course not. It is only when we walk around this city that we become aware that we are constantly climbing, descending, climbing again. Before, we assumed there was only one hill, the one where Notre Dame de la Garde sits enthroned. The Good Mother, who shines in the sun by day and under the flood-lights at night. Like an everlasting candle. Yes, Marseilles plays games with perspective. It's a tough climb to the old neighborhood, the Panier, up the steps of the Carmes. When you get to Place des Moulins, you discover you are as high as the Saint Charles Station, higher than the Church of the Réformes at the top of the Canebière, as high as Place Jean-Jaurès, known as the Plaine. And you start to imagine that from the pretty little houses surrounding the square you see the sea, always on both sides. Besides, in this neighborhood, which the Germans dreamed of razing to the ground in 1943, because its streets were so narrow that they couldn't keep control of it, when you come back down, by way of Rue de Lorette, Rue du Panier or Rue du Refuge, the terraces of all the houses compete with one another, some of them hurriedly arranged directly on the red tiles of the roofs. Here, there are hours of the day when you love feeling as if you are standing halfway between the light and the sea. It is a way of telling yourself once again, as every Marseillais will explain, why you are from here and not from somewhere else, why you live here and not elsewhere.

To linger in the Panier is to feel the old heart of Marseilles throbbing. A heart that speaks the languages of the world, the languages of exile. It is surely no coincidence that Pierre Puget, the architect, too little known as a painter, built the most beautiful building in this city: the Charité (the old Charité, as the Marseillais call it). Out of love for the neighborhood where he was born. That may well be why the Panier resists renovation, why it refuses to become the Montmartre of Marseilles that it was earmarked as. The neighborhood has been beautified, of course. And everyone is pleased about that. But unconsciously, those who live in it want to prolong its old history. "It's always been like this," they will tell you in any café.

The Treize Coins, for example. And they will add, in case you haven't understood, "Aren't we fine just like this, my friend?" It is on the other hill, the hill of the Plaine, in the streets close to Cours Julien, which have also been renovated and restored, that what was dreamed of for the Panier has actually happened. Not that this is Montmartre either. It's just Marseilles in a different register. The boutiques of Marseillais fashion designers rub shoulders with bars and restaurants, art galleries and antique shops stand next to jazz clubs, blues clubs, ragga clubs. But the nearby Place Notre-Dame-du-Mont has not changed its habits. A working-class square that seems to ignore the hustle and bustle that overcomes Cours Julien every afternoon. Here, too, we look out over Marseilles. A glance at Rue Estelle, which descends steeply only to come back up in a gentle slope on the other side. And even Cours Julien has to be reached by climbing Rue d'Aubagne. After crossing Rue Longue-des-Capucins. The street of the Eastern market. People say you don't smell the smells of Provence here. And it's true. Here, it smells like an Eastern port. The smells of the eternal Marseilles. You have to breathe them in, at least once. To become dizzy with the spices and the beauty of the women who come here to do their shopping. To take the time to argue with the vendors, who all come from the other side of the Mediterranean. This street, like Rue d'Aubagne, at the end on the left, before you get to the old Halle Delacroix, is a voyage along the Mediterranean, from Istanbul to Tangier. It is there that we feel—really feel—that the two shores have been responding to each other for centuries. It is when we have admitted that Marseilles is as eastern as Beirut is Latin that the apparent urban disorder of this city will disappear for the confused traveler. That he—you—will start to feel the sheer happiness of being here for one day, one week, or one month. Or forever, perhaps. And that's when you will discover the sea. And the bay. Vast and beautiful. Probably the most beautiful in the world, after the Bay of Naples. You will then understand

why Cézanne wore his eyes out painting L'Estaque. Why
Rimbaud came to die here, at the end of his travels, having
tired of poetry and men. Why, today just like yesterday, the
true journey can only begin here. Marseilles remains a gate-
way to the East. By following the sea, you will discover
neighborhoods and villages with romantic names: Les
Catalans, Le Vallon-des-Auffes, Malmousque, the bridge of
the Fausse Monnaie, Le Prophète . . . Marseilles unreels
her nooks and crannies all the way to the Impasse des
Muets, in the little harbour of Callelongue. Your eyes can't
get over it. Once past La Madrague de Montredon, the arid
white rock makes you doubt you could still be in
Marseilles, in the eighth arrondissement of the second-
largest city in France. Then, inevitably, because you are
lost, you come to a halt in front of the orientation map that
faces the Riou Islands. The land of the Big Blue. The noise
of the city, her exuberance, comes to an end here. In this
landscape that resembles the Aeolian islands. The silence
that falls over you, barely disturbed by the *phut-phut* of the
fishing boats returning from the open sea, is tangible. Salt
and iodine. Then, as you have, of course, forgotten to wear
walking shoes, you sit down calmly on a rock, behind an
angler. Time is abolished. In other words, it is all yours.
You may catch the angler talking to the fish. You may
catch yourself saying out loud your dreams of being elsewhere. Ulysses will become a reality. And you will be
proud to have discovered it. Returning to the city center,
after eating a pizza in the harbor of Les Goudes, you will
have discovered the truth about Marseilles. A truth
expressed in terms of sun and sea. She is perceived by the

heart through a particular carnal flavor that is all her bit-
terness and her grandeur. From Algiers, you will then hear
the voice of Albert Camus whisper in your ear: "The love
we share with a city is often a secret love."

FABIO MONTALE

FABIO MONTALE'S CHRISTMAS DINNER[3]

[3] A short work of fiction featuring Izzo's Fabio Montale, hero of the Marseilles trilogy. First published in *Regards*, issue 19, December 1996.

I'd promised myself I'd do it on Christmas Day. Visit Joëlle in prison. Take her a gift. Talk to her. Above all, talk to her. Five years ago, when I was still a cop, she'd killed her eighteen-year-old boyfriend, Akim. Stabbed him three times. With no motive. Except her fear. She killed him after making love with him. I never managed to get a single sentence from Joëlle. A single word. In her diary, she had written: "What did I do to be scared?!" And later: "It isn't the ordinary kind of fear that sometimes catches you unawares, or even the fear of ridicule that makes you clasp tight to your love, it's a deep fear, a fear without end." Between herself and her fear she had created a gulf: death. Murder. The murder of the man she loved most in the world.

I remember that when I handed Joëlle over to her judges, I told myself: human behavior is not logical, and crime is human. Then I stopped thinking about it. I avoided thinking, reflecting. In my head, I'd closed all the books that try to give meaning to our actions. And I kept myself away from all sensible reflections. I went fishing, I strolled through the *calanques*, I spent time cooking for a few friends, and devoted myself to drinking some good bottles of Provence wine.

"Hey, are you listening to me?" Fonfon said. He had just uncorked a bottle of white wine. From Puy Sainte-Reparade. I'd brought back twenty liters.

"Yeah."

"So Honorine and I decided to have our Christmas dinner together. She's alone, and so am I. Magali and the kids aren't coming. They're off doing winter sports."

A guy came to see us one day, at the Police Academy. A sociologist. Director of the National Center for Scientific Research. He had written a book: *Customs and Moods of the French According to the Seasons.* This guy, Besnard I think he was called, told us that suicide and murder neither go together nor in inverse proportion. People kill others and kill themselves a lot in July, that was his theory. But, he said, December is when suicide is at its rarest. He also told us that you don't find a corresponding rise in physical aggression in the onslaught of September, or a greater number of sex crimes in the depression of December. In both cases, according to him, the spring, until May, was a particularly quiet season for private violence. The explosion did not come until June. This guy had an explanation for all the questions a young cop might ask himself. It was great. A gun in one hand, a sociology book in the other. But Besnard had spoiled everything with his conclusion. "The seasonal variations in interpersonal violence," he declared, "do not seem to have a simple or spontaneous explanation, whether based on climatic conditions or the frequency of opportunity." Having analyzed everything, he had come back to his point of departure. Theory is no answer to any-thing. It just allows us to theorize. About murder. Rape. Delinquency. Even about road accidents. Instead of an approach based on the seasons, you could just as easily have an approach based on sex. Or on race. Everyone was trying to understand the world. By putting it into order. One day, everything had to find its order. And it was there that everything got complicated. No theory is correct until it has been verified. Just like scientific discoveries. The atomic bomb only became true after Hiroshima. Experimentation. The field of experimentation. Other modern applications had followed. The final solution envisaged by a chosen race. The gulag as the joy of the peo-ple. Sabra and Chatila as a preparation for peace. Bosnia. Rwanda . . . You always came back to the same starting point. To what had no meaning. To that moment without reason when a seventeen-year-old girl kills her boyfriend. "An unusual personality," the judge had said. Since then, Joëlle had withdrawn into silence. Forever. It was said she had gone mad. Because you need a word to describe the incomprehensible. Joëlle. One day. A long way from statis-tics. From the monthly variation in homicides. And the sea-sons. That was what you came back to. To fear. Life itself.

"I hate the snow," I replied.

"What are you talking about?"

"All right, I'll stay with you. What did you think, I was going to midnight mass?"

He smiled. "Honorine said she'd make us sea urchins, with a few oysters and clams as an appetizer. And the tra-ditional thirteen desserts to finish. The works!"

I took Fonfon by the shoulders and drew him toward me. With tears in my eyes. I started blubbering. I'd planned to visit Joëlle. But Joëlle hadn't waited for me. She'd killed herself the day before, at dawn. In her cell.

"It's all right," I said to Fonfon, straightening up. I let my gaze wander over the sea. Toward the horizon. I still haven't found any better way to forget the corruption of the world. Joëlle raised her eyes toward me. She had wonderful dark eyes. Could I have been a good father to her? Or a good lover? Could I have explained her fear to her? I nodded. As if to say yes. Yes, Joëlle. The farther you go into things, the more the difference between happiness and unhappiness becomes blurred. Yes, I could have explained that to you.

I knocked back my drink and stood up. I felt like going and losing myself in Marseilles. In her smells. In the eyes of her women. My city. I knew that I always had an appointment there with the fleeting happiness of exiles. The only kind that suited me. A real consolation.

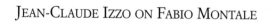

JEAN-CLAUDE IZZO ON FABIO MONTALE

I wrote the first book (*Total Chaos*) without knowing that I would write another. At the same time, I knew that I wouldn't write fifty. By the time I started *Solea*, I was already planning to put an end to Fabio Montale. (. . .) Obviously, there's a little bit of me in him. Personal things, values: the love of food and good wine, for example. On the other hand, I've always hated fishing . . . And I was never a cop. All the characters are invented. But they are based on friends . . . The only real one is Hassan, the owner of the Bar des Maraîchers. And the young people are my son and his circle of friends.

It's hard for me to analyze my success. I don't think I'm the kind of writer that everyone agrees about. There are some people who'll never read me . . . I don't make any concessions, either in form or content. I think my readers see themselves in the character of Fabio Montale and in the subjects of my novels, including relationship problems, and friendship, for example. Everyone sees Montale as the friend they have been looking for. (. . .) I'm often told my work is dark and pessimistic, but the nicest compliment I regularly receive is to be told that when people close *Solea* they have one hell of a desire to live! I find that touching, because it's the feeling I myself have when I read Jim Harrison. (. . .)

Yes, like Montale, I am a pessimist. The future is desperate. But I'm not the one who is desperate, it's the world . . . I say we can resist, transform, improve, but basically, we're stuck. We can't change anything fundamentally. On the other hand, in the space that we have, we can be happy.

I've stopped believing politicians who tell me that things will be better tomorrow, or that the revolution will change everything. (. . .) Everything I write about the involvement of the Mafia in the Provence and Côte d'Azur region is true. My past as a journalist must have something to do with it . . . (. . .)

Writing crime novels is not another form of activism. It's just a way of conveying my doubts, my anxieties, my joys, my pleasures. It's a way of sharing. Apart from my opposition to the National Front, I'm not trying to say: we must do this or we must do that. I just tell stories. If it spurs some people to join a group, so much the better. Montale doesn't belong to any party. He has values. He doubts. He's a lone wolf. But he does believe in a certain number of things.

As a citizen, as an activist, I no longer have much hope. But I still have a lot of hope in man. (. . .) Killing Montale in *Solea* is an alarm signal. If he represents hope, that means that, if you want other Montales, you have to do something about it . . .

FABIO MONTALE'S FAVORITE PLACES

Hassan's Bar des Maraîchers, on the Plaine.
Bar de la Marine, Quai de Rive-Neuve, in the Vieux-Port.
La Samaritaine, in the Vieux-Port.
Chez Ange, on Place des Treize Coins.
Bar des Treize Coins, on Rue Saint-François.
Chex Félix, on Rue Caisserie (Le Chaudron Provençal).
Chez Paul, on Rue Saint-Saëns.
Chez Mario, on Place Thiars.

FABIO MONTALE'S MUSIC

In *Total Chaos*:

Ray Charles, *What'd I Say* and *I Got a Woman* (Newport
    concert).
Miles Davis, *Rouge.*
Thelonious Monk

Calvin Russel: *Rockin' the Republicans* and *Baby I Love You* IAM.

Paco de Lucia, Django Reinhardt, Billie Holiday, Rubén Blades.

Lightnin' Hopkins, *Last Night Blues*.

Bob Marley, *Stir It Up*.

Paolo Conte.

Michel Petrucciani, *Estate*.

Astor Piazzolla & Gerry Mulligan, *Buenos Aires, Twenty Years After*.

Buddy Guy with Mark Knopfler, Eric Clapton and Jeff Beck, *Damn Right, He's Got the Blues*.

Dizzy Gillespie, *Manteca*.

Léo Ferré (at Hassan's Bar des Maraîchers).

In *Chourmo*:

Bob Dylan, *Nashville Skyline* and *Girl from the North Country*.

John Coltrane, *Out of This World*.

Miles Davis.

Bob Marley, *So Much Trouble in the World*.

Ray Barretto, *Benediction*.

Lili Boniche.

Los Chunguitos.

Art Pepper, *More for Less*.

Sonny Rollins, *Without a Song*.

Lightnin' Hopkins, *Your Own Fault, Baby, to Treat Me the Way You Do*.

Edmundo Rivero, *Garufa.*
Carlos Gardel, *Volver.*
ZZ Top, *Thunderbird*, *Long Distance Boogie* and *Nasty Dogs and Funky Kings.*

In *Solea*:

Miles Davis, *Solea.*
Mongo Santamaria, *Mambo Terrifico.*
Pinetop Perkins, *Blue After Hours.*
Lightnin' Hopkins, *Darling Do You Remember Me?*
Abdullah Ibrahim, *Zikr* (in *Echoes from Africa*).
Fonky Family, *Le Troisième Oeil.*
Nat King Cole & Anita O'Day, *The Lonesome Road.*
Gianmaria Testa, *Extra-Muros.*
Rubén González, *Amor Verdadero*, *Alto Songo*, *Los Sitio'Asere* and *Pio Mentiroso.*

FABIO MONTALE'S BOOKS

Within the Tides and *Lord Jim* by Joseph Conrad.
Grand Suitcase Hotel by Christian Dotremont.
Exile by Saint-John Perse.
The Marseilles poets Emile Sicard, Toursky, Gérald Neveu, Gabriel Audisio, and Montale's favorite, Louis Brauquier.